What Happens

University of Nebraska Press | *Lincoln*

What Happens

Poems

Hilda Raz

SET IN MINION PRO BY
SHIRLEY THORNTON.
DESIGNED BY A. SHAHAN.

Contents

Preface

Readers will find in these pages a daughter, Sarah. She was born in my twenty-sixth year, a familiar transformation of one woman into two parts. She was called Sarah after her father's grandmother, who'd raised him; he'd followed after her during his first hot summer, holding her skirts to learn to walk, calling for *ice, ice*. Sarah was our second child and at the time of her birth nothing seemed more important to me as a writer and teacher than engagement with female identity through generations. In the next decade I began to write this book.

Robert Pack, poet, critic, and then director of the Bread Loaf Writers' Conference, chose this book for publication in the Grove Press poetry series just as the press was changing ownership and the series was canceled. The manuscript fell into two parts: Judith Kitchen, editor of State Street Press, took one part for her series of chapbooks and published it as *The Bone Dish*; Eloise Fink chose the other for her Thorn Tree Press, where it was published as *What Is Good*. Both books are out of print. The original manuscript, called *What Happens*, was put away.

In the middle of my life, my daughter Sarah disappeared. The poems that traced her in the context of an ordinary life—the poems of female inheritance—had become unavailable in ways both literal and metaphorical. I continued to write and publish books—poetry and others—that redefined transformation: first in my own body because of breast cancer, *Divine Honors*, and then in the body of my younger child, *Trans*, both published by Wesleyan University Press. My daughter Sarah had become my son Aaron.

After Aaron's sex change, he and I wrote a prose book together, *What Becomes You*, published in the American Lives series by the University of Nebraska Press. The book describes our experience, asks questions about the nature of identity, and reveals details of

Aaron's sex change. And then another book of poems, *All Odd and Splendid*, again published by Wesleyan UP, pushed my ideas and poems forward.

Although I missed Sarah, who had gone from my life, I'd come to understand that my daughter was a construction — not of flesh but of words. She lived in this book. So when the University of Nebraska Press brought the parts back together and asked to publish *What Happens*, I said yes, with thanks. I hope readers will be as happy to meet Sarah here in our life and landscape as I am to have made her.

What Is Good originally was dedicated to John Franklin, Sarah, and Dale, and had these names and dates on the dedication page:

Franklyn Emmanuel Raz 1899–1957
Barton James Raz 1928–1968
Dolly Horwich Raz 1899–1969

The order of poems has been changed in service to the original manuscript.

Thank you to Robert Pack, Judith Kitchen, Eloise Fink, Ladette Randolph, and Tom Swanson for their support of this book.

What Happens

What Happens

one

one

That's Something

In Springfield, Nebraska
on the central flyway
in March, the geese
at sunset make such a ruckus
as you can hear for miles
either side of Highway 14
west or north on the gravel
marker roads, in the marshy
lowlands; you can park
and watch wave on wave
funnel and circle down
and down, peel off
from the main torrents
to land by what looks like
accident of blowing air
on farm pond or lake,
hog wallow, or bathtub,
or corn stubble or milo field—
to sleep.

All this, mind you,
against a black dish
of fiery sky that erases
detail and depth and leaves
these cutouts in the air,
scarcely geese at all
except where the final light
flashes pure white on their bellies
almost, not quite yet,
touching the water.

Jan's Orchard

Anything anyone human
might want of an evening
we've carried from the hold
of the station wagon
parked at the foot of the hill.
We loll on the grass and drink.

A spring orchard in Stella,
even the blasted trees blooming,
pear, cherry, and apple,
and we're eating a picnic supper
and drinking wine in the middle
under an umbrella of blossoms.

The sun at the horizon
catches rose in our glasses.
We say nothing.
If the good life is coming
to us in our lifetime,
surely it is here
in this orchard in April at twilight,
everything possible blooming,
the air — impossible — warming
as the sun goes down.

Everything here is becoming
summer if we let it,
three people who try hard
to drink and keep this air down
on the ground among grass blades,
while it bubbles and rises
and floats us, finally,
our pale quilts and jackets,
our jokes and stories,
into the night sky,
shrinking and whirling us
higher and higher
until we're dust motes,
no, lightning points,
no, star folds,
nothing around us cold,
nothing around us, no,
we are nothing
but sighing over the flowers.

What Happens

In Alma, Nebraska, at midnight
into a spring storm the young doctor
goes out. He says he is going
to deliver the widow's baby.
I am sitting in the parlor
with my new friend, our landlady,
who is painting my nails
what she calls *a good color*.
She paints her own and tells
the story of the widow.
Outside the window the rosy snow
comes down on the crocus.

Diction

"God is in the details,"
I tell the kids
in the public school
at Milligan, Nebraska.
They wonder what I mean.
I tell them to look
out the window
at the spring fields
the mud coming up
just to the knee
of the small pig
in the far pasture.
They tell me
it's not a knee
but a hock
and I hadn't ought
to say things I know
nothing about. I say
the light on the mud
is pure chalcedony.
They say the mud
killed two cows
over the weekend.
I tell them the pig
is alive and the spring
trees are standing in a green haze.
They tell me school is out
in a week and they have to plant.
The grain elevator at the end
of Main Street stretches out
her blue arms. The kids say chutes.

The Sandhills, Early Winter

The girl in the back row sits perfectly still,
doesn't answer my unspoken question
about her pajama top, why she wears it
as a blouse today in school, fifth period
when I teach her class, or why her eye
is bruised shut, her glasses broken
in the same lens, her skin cut.

Or why her paper is tattooed with hearts
and arrows, broken in places under the ink,
for yesterday's lesson,
but today's is blank and she's slumped

when I bend over her to brush the page
with my palm and ask questions
the other kids hear, about sounds and smells,
the texture of wind on gravel, on hard ice.

But as I move on, she bends to write
what I'd rather not read
in my gym corner office behind the stage
and later I wave in the face of the principal.
I read her lines out loud and when I'm finished,
he says a sentence coupling nouns and verbs
in a way I've never heard before
and ends by saying, "No,
No, we've tried, we can't do anything."

That night I buy her a bus ticket
out of there, drive fifty miles to the Greyhound
station and click her seatbelt shut before the motor starts

and again, a plane ticket for where it's warm
and the close sun heals
and take her home to my daughter's room
I drive to her trailer house in the country and when
her uncles and father come to the door
her brothers behind them, I smile and say
I'm the visiting teacher and we've got a problem

and on Friday, as always, I'm out of there.

November Night Driving

You can't find the brights
so when the deer flush from the ditch
we catch only the fists of their tails
as they turn, swerve away
from the front end where I sit stunned
twenty feet from their hard haunches.

All day I have been following
snow geese so high in masses
against flat sky
only pattern can be
the eye's subject.
Tonight the thud and rush of deer
pulled onto pavement
by legs so thin they are poles
pushing boats
through dark waters.

Now I see them
particular, clear,
a near miss, buff and flesh.

Birthday

You made a small grey dish of clay,
glazed it something purplish
and filled it, years later,
with minute bones, perfectly intact
you delivered with your scalpel thumbnail
from an owl pellet: scapula, mandible,
four perfect teeth the size of seeds,
and pieces of a backbone ladder,
all pure matte white, "from a mouse,"
you said, pushing up your glasses.
We sat looking, forehead to forehead.
The air was steamy. The shaggy residue
went, swept to the floor by an elbow,
but the rest is here where I sit by the window
on my birthday, looking out, missing you
daughter, preserver, maker, eyes.
I stroke the bone dish and write this down.

Sarah's Wing

On the teak table,
bare except for a spring primrose
brought home from the grocery,
is a wing. I've never seen it before.
It's copper-enameled,
called cloisonné, turquoise and jet,
lapis lazuli, coral: the colors, she calls
from the kitchen, of Egypt; and it's etched
on the reverse, where the feather spines
would lie, if they were real, flat
against the frail skin. The wing.
The wing she made so small
I can hold it in my palm,
a perfect pretender:
her amulet.

She is my wing.

Conversation

My daughter calls long-distance
about a Binturong, to say
it smells like popcorn; imagine
(she went on Sunday to the zoo)
this animal! And she wants
a pomegranate and some kiwi fruit
(the last were rotten) and that sausage,
and the Loeb Library's *Natural History*
(Pliny) in twelve small volumes
for her Wednesday birthday,
through the mail; and did I know
women's hands were small once
smaller than ours, and men short
but twice as wide as her father is?

She's looking for an overcoat to wear
and gloves for her wall—old ones—
and her heat bill was a hundred dollars,
is that too much? She waits. I wait too.
The phone weather blows the bars,
this freezing distance, farther apart.

My Daughter Home from College Tells Me about the Gods

Ra, whose chariot they ride
over us by day
under by night, is
in the Unworld. They are Pharaohs
or their indispensable retainers
named in advance on the tomb walls
thus guaranteed a place
in the sun boat.

She kneads dough
while she talks
then rolls and folds
the long loaves.

Horus, who is both one
God and another . . .

The bread rises under a linen cloth.

She says human longing for mystery
leads to a commonality of belief
in immortality;

and who is to know, she asks,
patting the loaves onto a cornmeal tray,
whether the unburned woman
isn't really impervious to fire.
Isn't it belief in the fire that makes us burn?

April Teaching, Outstate

A week in Gere, seven hours down the Interstate in fog.
Then double snow days—no school, who would believe it.
Women's coffee at the house of the Supt. (he's gone).
His wife is fiery but banked; his children are blond.
What he is there's a word for, but I don't know it.
When I leave, he hands me a check, strokes my throat,
Asks near my ear if his handsome face isn't enough payment.

All week, all night I am restless under an electric blanket.
The snow melts by my window. The grandfather clock,
made by an uncle, chimes against the bed wall
where my head is, telling each hour, each half,
the divisions a loud ruler measuring
something I'd rather not note

not here, not now as the snow thaws
shiny in the street gutters, pouring above leaf rot
silver runnels into low places that jar
my car as I skid away from the new school for little kids
to the high school where what waits
is hardly friendly, that old spring enemy
stirring everywhere in them, in me, in the deep running
recesses of these heavy bodies we wear
and hesitantly touch to the sunlight again.

At the end of the hour, incoming seniors grunt and rush
to throw open the windows, they say the room stinks
like a gym where we've been working-out;
they teeter on the frames, lean and breathe in the air.

Native

You tell about the soldier,
"who gave button polish to a savage
who knew little about cures
for his sick infant.
And the child died," you report
in the tone of the scout
writing down in his book
the events of the day.

Someone gave you the book.
It is old and the scout
according to the ways of the world
has stopped writing.
He is cleansed of the world
and floats near the child
on the crest of the air.

Only the painted father is left
stalking the grasslands
watching our footfalls
sharpening his weapons
on the stones of his fields.

Locus

8 a.m.
Bach variations on harpsichord.
Cat puts head
into huge cluster
of peach colored
unarranged peonies
in stoneware vase
less open at top
then center where it bulges.
Pale sun
over my shoulder
falls and glows
on teak tables.

Looking up
I see the shout
of a cardinal
sitting exactly on top
the new leader
of the forty-year-old
blue spruce,
who stays
long enough
for me to consider
calling out.

Just as
tree
beast
flowers
bird
become with light
a natural blessing,
a sudden absence
of any sound
resolves completely
the exhausted music.

Accident

High summer heat.

Here clear storage bags
from a strange kitchen
hang upside down
from chrome hooks
high in the air over a bed
where someone I know
who resembles someone precious
is lying naked. It wears blue
hoses in its throat.

Air makes a sound it makes
nowhere else. What is lying
on the bed is breathing,
surely now absorbing
red threads at all
the body's openings.
I can't stay here very well.
I can't stay here long.

No flowers allowed.

They go in
they come out of the far room
where air is frigid.
They say *rigid*, they say *fluid*
they say something
I can't hear.
I'm not listening.

Light comes and goes.
I go into the room, I come out.
I say something again and again.
His toes are cold.

Going away coming back
trees unfurl
in an arch over some oval.
My hands and feet move together
and I move
into the arch
as the oval moves out.

He smiles
around tubes.
I smile.
He is sitting up in a cage.
He can't talk. He has a hose
in his throat.
His dials leap.
"Is this the worst from now on?"
he writes on a board.
Now he is sleeping more deeply
than I can say. Surgery.
Now he is rescued.

Is he breathing?
Yes, quietly. He is sleeping,
breathing alone.

Now he is beginning to walk.
He is more tall than my womb
but very bending.
He leans on something chrome.

Now we are going home.
He is buckled into his seat,
dressed
he is sitting beside me.
I am buckled too.
We are going home.
I have been scrubbing his room.
I can polish its wood
I can shine its windows;
it has food. He enters it.

He is very thin.
He is slow down the hall.
Behind him, I can't see
he is breathing
and moving.

Twenty-one years ago
I panted and bore down
into scarlet and dazzle
between my thighs
in order to release him
to the shiny air

that tick-turning cord
still pulsing.

You
lift up from the bloody ditch
and watch
what's whole and dripping
come again into the world.

Photograph of a Child Sleeping

God is Good. It is a Beautiful Night.
Wallace Stevens

Blond head,
my lips lowered to brush it.

Brown bird,
your notes rise
and fall in the world
washed now by a skim of snow.
Sing sound in patterns
without meaning
so I hear.

We open the earth with spades
and enter it with our bodies,
or bulbs of tulip and crocus
that decay with years
or daffodils that bloom longer,

or amber, washed onto shores
with beetles preserved forever

not alive, not breathing, but intact,
surrounded, green and iridescent.

Where is sound rising
to meet spray,
sap hardened to a fist
only flame changes?
Where in the snow-scrim
is the bird you promised?

Bend close, fair head
to my milky breast
where you are nourished.

Visions

Three women in a niche
their robes verdigris; a pale moss
the color of bronze plushes the brick.
From their mouths the water of fountains dribbles,
darkens the cobbles, runs down and pools their bare feet.
An iron fence divides us from silver,
the copper luck of coins.

I dream about a fluent woman
trapped in a flood of language,
a living flux her body interrupts.
But into her is sluiced and out
a particular speech so balanced
she is a floodgate and from her mouth
the tamed waters flow and chant.

My son in his hospital gown,
flayed ribs raising the thin cotton
into a tent of air he breathes,
wakes from long sleeping.

A silent woman drowsing in a chair
his thin foot in my hand,
I startle at lightning.

He opens his blazing eyes.

The conduits of his body charge again.
Long filaments
lift from his perfect head
and sway like anemones
in bands of light
thickening the edges of his room
beneath the pale ceiling. Others,
sheer filaments, connect with, touch,
slot into and braid
an entire tough weave I know
keeps us, generation to generation, safe.
Waves of air rock the chrome bed frame
free of its straps and tubes
and his voice, unhinged from long silence,
rises in vowels he chants in counterpoint
with those in the niche of the saved.

Three women in a wet niche
their robes verdigris; a plush moss
like bronze clings to the brick.
Their mouths open in anguish
and out dribbles the fountain waters,
runs to and pools the cobbles at their feet
scaly with copper, the silver luck thrown in.

Words

Deft and *dexterous*, its sister,
are some so defined.
Meanwhile the air glisters,
no, that is water in the distance,
a warm bowl beckoning.

We are alive, hurrah,
unlike some precious others
and others, still anonymous,
whose life's work is done.
How to enjoy the moment, then,
the salve of breath unnoticed
and grief, waving its handkerchief
from behind a holly bush?

Or the ones gone
whose warm skin
nightly becomes
an embrace so habitual
as to be painful? We push them away, those
we most want:

orphans, women stranded at the front,
figures holding aloft other figures,
alive, human, in ruins, rubble
of human waste at their feet.

We grieve so quietly
how can we live properly?

Town/County

Beyond the city is the prairie.
Breathers there have found their places
in the tall, common grasses
on the land, intact in webby roots.

What crisis of decision comes
in the empty air of the city
doesn't matter. Meadowlarks and finches
hurl their voices across the ditches
in the silence of the summer wind
and speeding by, we hear them.

Or the wind wraps itself around our houses.
Some people complain of the leaves' noises,
their voices, but we notice little,
only our animals sitting in the windows
asking to come in, asking to be let out:
they hear the wind.

Or so I speculate over a cup of mango tea
brought, God knows how, from the tropics.
The brown kettle steams on a Japanese stove.
Padouk coasters protect the teak surfaces.
A Siamese cat sits on our knees
and outside, the prairie stiffens for winter.

two

owt

Dishes

Now is always still.
Antonio Machado

For years I have been doing the dishes.
Once, two months from giving birth,
I stood at the sink with my friend
(big with a child) who held lobsters,
one in each hand. They were shiny, black from the sea
and salty and would be sweet, later, in our mouths
and itchy to our bare forearms as we sat, one each side
of a crockery bowl, cracking shells, pulling meat
for the salad. But now they were struggling.
And I left off washing to reach out and take them,
laughing at their pegged claws and only a little afraid,
and watched her lift the deep lid from the steaming kettle.

Later, dinner. Music came across the lake
through the opened windows and air moved
on our wet skins, and we knew small burstings
of kernels torn from their cobs and deep ripples
behind our denim aprons as the babies who would soon be
daughters rolled and elbowed. And then the dishes.

We sat together on high stools at the soapstone sink
and washed our hands in pale suds, and dried them.
The piles of plates grew and were transported
away and then the deep orange enamel pots, heavy
in our shining hands. And then it was dark.

We put our dripping towels on the wooden dowel racks
and, as balanced as we could be on the rock steps,
lumbered down the slope to the shore. We dropped
our flowered cotton clothes where we stood in the grass
and naked, walked into a cool water as dark as our futures
where we floated and sank and turned up, calling across
a widening surface of silver water, calling
and whispering and calling, *sister, sister*.

What Happened This Summer

They put their heads on one side, and looked wise,
which is quite as good as understanding a thing,
and very much easier.
Oscar Wilde, *The Birthday of the Infanta*

A door slams.
"What is the message of the door?"
I ask in the dark. You don't know
and I don't know either but now
I tell you it meant goodbye.

From the shadows we made on the road,
longer than Giacometti women,
hooked shadows and no eclipse
of our bodies, light points. Above,
ordinary stars and a late moon.

"A few fireflies on the road,"
you said, "Look," and "look."

Saying Good-bye to the Property

On the first cold day in August
in a northern state,
the sun reflects on the gazebo
a lattice of light.

In the crevice of a rock in my path
forbidding farther progress
is a small pine in the shape of a feather.
It will not let go
though I pull on it, even to keep my balance.

Underfoot on the paths
I've wandered for years with the children
poison ivy flourishes.
They are grown into beauty
and the girls' breasts are like my own.

A quarrelsome age settles on us all
and on our parents
death shows a common face.
Not the red leaf
not the cry of the tern can hold me.

I will not come here again.

Divorce

You stand in the doorway saying
It's only a scab;
It's only a penny of blood.
Stop I say stop.

Then it's time for the suicide,
Daft, hitching his way down
the mountain. You don't ask,
How was his nose broken.

His head is opened by the bullet,
the knife you let fly,
the fight on the lawn, punch
Counterpunch.

Listen I tell you,
Stop. Anything can happen.

Shame,
or the Computer Uses of Natural Language

Sarah Stueber Bishop, *The Women's Review of Books*

Die
Option not listed
List Options
Run lie confess

Run: I head for the purple hills
whose coarse vegetation packs
the eye with color: vermillion,
the season being fall, and greens
in various shades, shapes, and textures.
Mud underfoot limns footsoles
on fallen trees, cool breezes
come down white into cones and rods:
a melding in this valley so low . . . *No.*

Lie: I have offended none, not the thief
whom I counseled in the distribution of goods;
not the woman crying silently in interstices
in the music, whose children eternally are
missing; not the woman counting her capital,
planning an order for the armorer;
not the scholar, whose excellent constructs
measure precisely the elegant dimensions
of the pasture, pegging down cerulean silk
at all corners; not the beggar to whom I offered
chilly amber, fresh from Baltic waters,
small pebbles blowing hard off the sand
at her belly. I have not done these things . . . *No.*

Confess: I have slender wrists.
Nothing excites me more than the mind
except it's the body. Where weather is,
I am, or in the pew with Henry James
behind the hostile but bereaved family.
He won't speak to me, and for good reason.
Today I have offended
A friend who is childless,
with talk of my children;
a friend who drank too much,
with chablis I took from a cup;
and a woman who saved me once
from the harsh absence grief demands,
come today with news and terror
I couldn't fight or succor,
whom I sent away with nothing
more than books and a cold supper.

The small birds balance on the mountain ash
again at dusk; nothing is altered.
The cat takes to the garden, rolls
on the hard earth. She is flesh to the ground.
Small yellow tomatoes suspended in air
from their upright vines. For centuries
the same five notes have come from the lark.
What can I do? Die? *Option not listed.* List options.

1 September, 100 Degrees

End of summer:
higher heat
only absence
of light lowers.
Louring sky.
Moon fourteen days
from full,
dry ground;
fissures
marigolds droop into.
Nothing's waxen, creamy.

Across the prairie
hot air blows
down gulleys;
city alleys
hold the heat,
their garbage cans
too fierce to touch
without a glove.
All beasts are fitful
come inside
except the mole
who dies on the patio
dripping babies.
We lift her
on a shovel
drop her in
just as the last one
falls away.

Trying to Buy Off Death

is no effort in the blue hours.
The feral cats feast in the garbage,
chicken bones that can kill them,
so good the cats don't die.
The whole fetid smell of the place.
Look, I say, look. I have a clean
business proposition for you.
Value in the vault. A real contract.
If I die, I say, you have none of my assets;
even my books are gone.
My small, aristocratic feet
up the flue.

With this thousand you can have
Mexico,
with this one, kid boots of
a charming softness.
And the last, the best,
pays off the death car, color of mourning.

See, now the sun is trying to rise.

I Can't. Yes, You Can.

Listen to the rain
draping her sheet corners
over the roof edge, tucking
into the least cracks of the house
not only tight damp but overflow,
a plethora of water
to drown, no, to float
what? dust into the mud collars
around the new hydrangea,
the coleus, the hosta
in their raised beds of railroad ties.

The cat? The cat twists her head
as you do, hearing in rain
more than breath, less than
the torrential music of the tropics
where you lay once in a bunk
tucked under his bulk, listening
to the houses sway and sigh
in their hammock of banyan.

Deep night again. Awake.
All the children gone.
The loud thunder muttering
under her lightning cloak,
tightening her collar,
Where are they, where *are* they?

In their marble perimeters
the mothers lie still. Water
silkens their earth. In their cradles
of bone they sleep, their silence
the ground for thunder, deep rumble
of voices they no longer hear.

Under her hill of belly
some woman flexes her toes,
shifts her weight to straighten her spine,
hears her breath: in, out, stop,
then sinks into the opening of her body,
thunder, the crack of lightning
beginning to show hair, an oval of hair.

Where am I? Dark and thunder
lightning and rain. The cat.
I breathe so deeply only I can hear.
The children's doors stand open.
Their rooms are bare.

The sheet of the rain
covers my house,
tucks into corners
a film of skin, a patch.
I stay inside and watch for morning.

Worry about Meaning

What if I'm broken and can't be mended,
or worse, the world is broken around me
and I the only whole thing in it?

The light at the window fractures to get in.
Trees in their winter doldrums, dun and silver,
static as desks, seem one thing, now another.
How to say the difference?

The doorbell, the alarms of the clock, the shatter
and stutter of tableware, what do they mean to us
eating and drinking with family who come from our bodies?
Our pets on the floor animate, lungs
rising and falling in lucid continuum
above their rounded bellies. Oh Lord, you've collapsed

time for us so the moment of conception,
its fluids and contortions,
exists at the moment the water breaks on tile,
splashes the shoes of the attending intern,
and the same child brought forth
is off in a flurry of tatters and knits and leathers.
Why are the perfumes of the inner and outer body
filled with the smells of earth?
The prairie grasses, those healing sponges under our feet,
push up our shoe soles in patterns not particular, not saving.

On the tarmac, we hunch over weapons,
can't wait for the bloodflow to slow,
be staunched, for membranes to reach out
minute fibers of muscle,
silver under a dribble of fluids,
and ease, thin, scar over, meet.

Cradle

I buy a watercolor of a woman
on a bed. She is naked.
I call her mother. Her nourishing breasts
shine in light from an invisible window.

A woman sits on a bed in light.
She is far away. She is more perfect
than formal matter.
Her hands are working clay.
Life into life, plunging hands
into a tub half filled with water.
Pink light falls steadily onto her shining shoulders,
this light in my mind.

When I leave I turn mother-woman to the wall.
No man there likes her,
her large breasts, her mysterious closed eyes.
She is heavy. She is an other.
I am only slightly other, lean and narrow
front to back, side to side.
When I say, "I feel," they smile.
Mother-woman is silent. She is a painting.

The men are lean, their body hair
a tender fur at crotch and armpit; front to back
their flesh close to long bones.
I cup my palm to the backs of their heads.
I touch the skin over their skulls.

A pale fur
hugs the long bones of their bodies,
narrow bones cradled close to my nourishing breasts.
A blond beard catches light.
What does it mean, this soft flesh above my ribs?

Mother-woman's breasts rest on the hard cradle of her ribs,
her softness under my skull.
Where are my children,
my large-breasted daughter, my solid son?
Where have they taken their bones
that grew in my center like clay, the slough of the very air?
They have walked them away, cradled in flesh.

The watercolor picture of mother-woman
calls me. Child, she says,
flesh is its own calling.
Your flesh is a cradle.
You live there in the glow of your bones.
Be at ease. I am with you.

Family

The famous poet is sitting, she
is sitting in a wicker lawn chair
drawn down by her arms to the head
of her Dalmatian, unnamed on this book jacket.

One could ask someone, a friend
of the poet, not—as I am—a friend of the work.
I don't know her nor am I likely to, except
through the clear language covering
breast and genitals in her poems.
Everything stirs, always, in the final stanza
but what comes before is static, passion
in disguise under a cotton tunic flushed
toward pink at the armholes. Her poems
have no flowers in their arms, don't tell us
hold on tight, won't call us names
we won't claim no matter how we want to;
our faces and noses reject the restraint
of high forehead, middle-German flesh
packed in fresh skin, jut of heavy bone frame.

This woman cooks, she preserves, she leads horses by the reins
through the mushroom woods, makes rot into omelets
redolent of basil, herbs grown not on the windowsill
but in their own plot behind the larger kitchen garden
where horse droppings are forked under
in service to what turns air to fire.

In the picture she sits, head lowered to the dog.
I love this woman and lower my head to her,
to rest on her text, rest my arms
(arms that flower into hands, on their center fingers
the pale mine-cut diamonds of my dead mother)
on the pink jacket of her new book.

Piecing

No woman in my family sews
but Nana jumped down a well
to save my mother, the sickly one
they say fell in. And once,
homesick for her Russian village,
she took up babies and jewels, stitched
gold in a chamois sack between her breasts,
and set out from England, a runaway.
The oldest, not yet four,
remembered smothering underneath
a quilt while Nana slept, head down
on that duvet of her tiny daughters.
The border guards weren't fooled.
They did what any Prussian would
and sent for Papa. Of course he came.
Next year they had a son.
Later that Russian village burned to the ground.

Gram, my father's mother, the beauty
of New York City in the nineties, said,
"For women, only good names matter."
Not a soft spot in the perfect body
she wore beneath boned corsets
until grandchildren put her underground
at eighty. At twenty, she told her husband,
youngest son of the richest man in town,
her gates were locked, they'd stay that way.
She kept the children, sold the mansion
and bought a grocery store she worked enough
to push the kids through school,
tied off, sold out, and folded at forty,
still colorful, strait laced and blonde.
She didn't remarry, said she didn't care for men

except her sons, Daddy—but fifteen years younger—
her favorite until he died before she did.
Her only daughter worked the books in a car wash to support her
and a frail husband, had no children
lost the name I took back and try to carry on.

My own mother, no handiworker, nevertheless left me
an unworn grosgrain ribbon dress she wove,
no doubt at great expense: two years worth of pastime.
I refused to take it home. Her name is gone, her sisters dead.

Shall I stitch here Mother's damask sofas,
matching wing chairs, Morris wallpapers, hall brasses
she collected instead of horses (she was terrified of horses)?
Which words to appliqué her whole again
upon an English woolen from her favorite robe?
No silk can fill her paneled hall with light
or patch her shadow on that slate.

As Nana sixty years before
climbed over the stone lip of the well
to save her, so Mother, pricked
by a stiffening palsy into stasis,
woke one morning early in her rented bedroom,
turned without noise to wake her sister
caretaker in the other bed,
put on her silk wrapper, tied the cord,
shuffled to a high-backed chair with arms
—one of twelve she'd shipped from the big house—
and dragged it over the Turkish carpet to the balcony doors,
weighted to keep them level in the wind,
and pulled them open on the ocean view,
a curled iron railing, slick with rain.

She dragged the chair,
and stopped to rest,
then climbed, stood, and breathed the damp,
and jumped and fell.
"Blunt trauma," said the certificate
that came home with her body.

This morning rising early,
broken ribs in a binder, ten pounds heavy,
I see in the mirror both the fine, full body
of my daughter, away at school,
and Mother there, intact inside her perfect skin.
I thank her. I begin to piece; I take up pen.

Plate xii

*A series of seventy original illustrations to Captain Sir
R. F. Burton's Arabian Nights, in oils, specially painted
by Albert Letchford, London, H. S. Nichols Ltd., 1897.*

O I confess I am small.
Smaller than a thread.
Smaller than a thread of pond ivy scum.
Than the bead of light on a thread of algae,
the split underside of a beetle,
its iridescent least leg scale.

Before your might
I am tears on your tile floor.
A bead of sun at the carpet edge,
the rose thread of the maker's sign
in fringe turned under by the layer's knee,
he in his big apron kneeling
on a day you don't enter
your lavish, your least reception room.
His leather knee patch.
I am nothing fresh.

You nod in passing,
set trembling bells
on your vest edge, their musical calling
freshening air you walk through
your hand swirling air in its least blessing.
I stand back in fear. I tremble at the edge
of the vast corridors you pass through.
I tremble in the hair-like cilia of the inner ear whorl
of your least subject who sinks to his knees
before you as you pass.
Before your wrath I am less than he.
I am less than he is.

I am less than your camel driver's fingernail.
Less than your draper, your linen draper
who pries open the long teak drawers
to raise out the heavy layers, the lengths of your linen,
who wraps your head in their waxy scents,
who catches in the folds of your crinkly beard
this fingernail and tweaks, your frown he covers and drapes over,
your fine deep alabaster forehead
covered and wrapped in creamy folds, your cool linen headdress.
I am less than the fray in the golden cord
he wraps your head with.
I am cut off and dropped away.

I fall to the tile floor.
Less than a metal thread, less than a single twist of flax,
less than the scour cloth in your sweet-jar,
less than the sour rag in the palm of your least cook,
that she-servant, I am less than the base metal clip
on your least concubine's braid,
the tie that binds her hair closed,
the tin button on her jerkin you undo,
the thread gives way, the clatter, less than her shudder,
less than the gleam on the oily knife hilt,
the blade entering,
less than her cry, less than yours.

Assignment

You say write
a poem about grief
but how can I
when snow outside
the window muffles
everything?
Falling onto
the cold of the kitchen
floor in the middle of the night
often, one terrible winter?
Is that how the poem begins?
Or riding to the cemetery
in the famous dark car
of my mother's brother,
the surgeon, who insists
on asking impossible
and rude questions about
the suicide of my brother?
They're all dead now,
what does it matter?

No, something about taking off
in an airplane on the way
to someplace healing, how the
runway splintered, all that silent
dashing around in the head bent
first over one bed, then another,
pushing aside the breathing tubes,
brushing the ivs, propping up
heads bending back blankets,
smoothing the sheets, pushing
hair back with the flat of my palm,
touching with lips the damp foreheads,

all that saying good-bye while the plane
jumped up, *thunk*, with no effort
and bounced, a lurch in the belly,
back onto the ground, and took off.
And I said good-bye.

Three Ways of Looking at It

Having been given permission to write
hooks into the soft portions of cheeks
I write this down on a morning of trees
cracked, chimneys felled, decimation
the old way, by lot, limbs torn from trunks,
sockets exposed; stumps partially
uprooted, fracture everywhere
no glistening, no green haze:
hopeless December, month of death
like all the others.

Tension demands a second stanza
whose blossoms toss on branches
upward into the summer air
in the fists of lovers
whose gesture signifies triumph,
union. Even the sun is singed, fused
with the blazing sky.

And I am sitting in a neutral season,
autumn in the window, washed now and
again by shudders of wind,
now the throat catch, the faltering
lungs, now the heart beating
triumphantly if irregularly loud:
see me, see me sitting here,
still alive, see this ordinary
impermanent, failed winner?

three

three

Gossip

*The little things may be none of
our business but we like them.*
Bernice Stole

At lunch she tells the story of an old lover
and his ten-year-old son, all canoeing
on the Swift River. Two took off their shirts
in the heat of work and swagger, to leave her
on the front seat bailing water and tidying gear.
Was she singing? Surely yes, and tucking up
her escaping hair in its pink bandana.
Sweat hung from her earlobes and its salt
mustached her upper lip. She was angry.

All at once her shirt with its oblongs
of damp at front and back, like open castanets
but blue and still, came off, she took it off
deliberately, they didn't see her fingers
reaching for the final, embroidered buttonhole
or the shine of her left shoulder shrugging,
or smell sweat running from her drying armpits,
her breasts, like theirs in air, the sun warm
on her hair as she shook off the square cloth,
stood up, and no one anywhere in the boat
said anything.

Father

is never home but she loves him —
adores him, really, and so does Mom:
his big, burly body, his flannel shirts,
woolens over interesting scars
with stories to tell. Oh, he is a raconteur
with racks of bottles in the fragrant breakfront.

He tells her not to talk so much.
His talk holds the world intact;
when it stops, the key piece
drops out the bottom and the whole
plastic globe fragments. Nothing's
the same ever again.

The size of him! The size of them all,
uncles, cousins, the brothers:
wide shoulders jutting through cigar smoke
in the breakfast nook. The deep black marks
of their synthetic heels never quite scrub out.

Under the huge dining table,
under the carpet where his big feet wait,
is the bell. When he pushes it with his shoe
an aunt, or mother, or a maid
brings out another dish
from the steaming kitchen.

But he paid for it, paid for it all,
sweaters, teak tables with brass inlay,
steaks, furs, wicks for the memorial
candles, silk stockings, full tin box
the color of sky, plants
and their white rings on the mahogany,
and the cars, deep greens, metallic,
and the cashmere lap-robes,
and the aunts and out-of-work uncles.

He was best loved, best beloved in the family,
whose very shadow, even absent,
absorbed all color, sucked short
the seasons, colored grey
even the lavish lilacs of that northern city

she never visits. She sends money
to an old woman who tends the graves,
sends money when the penciled bills come in.

Women Raised in the Fifties

Someone in my dream
says she likes my earring
over and over again
outside the window
the wren watches the cardinal
preen. Water in the birdbath
draws light to it.
My daughter praises the grace
and beauty of her stepmother's "face
and carriage." I look in the mirror.
From the far room, laughter.
Men through the door
beckon, say something to live for.

She

There is health in brown and too much talk in silver.
Frederick M. Link

I met an old woman once
who blabbed her theories,
not a one grounded in fact,
or if so she didn't say,
and though she made clear
the details, what she called,
"layers of transparencies
that hide or comprise
history, the universe and art,"
the while she talked—
an afternoon through, and an evening—
her famous husband watched in the background
or hid his eyes in his glass.

When I dream or lie waking
my mind fills with snippings
I swear if you asked me
I couldn't speak them plain.
But next day in the garden
lines overlap with the squares
until the map of the bulbs
resembles my moving mind.

At lunch last week my old friend
leaned on his elbow and said
the reason we get along so fine
is that he talks forever on
about himself and I'm still,
never liking to say who I am.
I notice the clear cellophane of his face
clipped at the edges, his blue eyes.

When I was a child my daddy
left often on business.
I'd cry for hours, yes, thrash
on the floor wanting him home
to cure the quiet.

I dig my garden
our garden my husband turns under
with mulch. All winter
we lie on our quilt circling
the catalogues, talking new husbandry,
fat bulbs packed with life
I imagine tucked up but waiting to spring
loose in the border soil
he trucked in.
He circles daylilies on paper,
maroon with gold centers.
I don't like them. No, I like them too.

For sixteen years I've saved up
for special occasions, felt my body
brush loose
silk of my holiday dress.
In my hands
the paintbrush feels alive with color.
Pencil lines
over the cream primer on the canvas
guide me right
so what comes out is floral, almost
an exact replica of how lilies
bloat in the wind then bend.
Their powdery pollen once stained
my linen skirt. My large hands
brushed the silvery light, brushing it off.

What Is Good

The banks of rivers
and rivers
and river dells
and patches of shade
in trees we swing from.
The grasses in winter,
their colors and swirls.
The birth
and the recovery
and the long swaths
we make walking in uncut grass.
The fields to the horizon.
The horizon like a bowl.
Clay we scrape up
and carry home and wedge.
The potter's wheel
spinning. And its noise,
a ground in great music
we write. We write great music.

The shells we gather, the soft bodies
of their tenants swept to sea
or buried. The ice houses in poems
of the salt sea. The tingling of hand
and dipped arm. And the swell
and the dip of the salt.
The mounds of casings
left by armies
and the bones buried in shallow graves.
The celluloid film we expose to light
and our flickering images in dark.
The baleen of whales, their cartilage,
and the brackish residue strained out between.
Foam. An eddy.
Our soft bodies and their phosphorescence,
their smoke.

Kid slippers, each toe a hollow,
and the dance card. Teeth filled
with molten gold. Gold in a case.
The rising of sun
and its going down in books,
in strips of house windows,
and the hollow of the groin
fitted to another one.
The high shale falls
and their engorgement, their waters
a great weight. And the perfect egg.
The breath we take in
and exhaust. The dead,
honeycombed with rot. Their ashes.
Commemorative fires in brass trenches.
The ground. The ground.

Lot's Wives

He frees himself by not caring
about the consequences.
If she turns, he loses her.
He looks toward the distant wife
drawing near, their child
in her fair arms. He is happy.

Never has he been so happy,
no never, not in the first days
of this double marriage.
The dark wife recedes as he moves
forward. He doesn't care.
Behind her their children, grown now
he tells anyone who'd listen, follow.
Their mother, he says, is freed by their leaving.

He doesn't care.
He says he has done his part
waking at dawn on one body, now another.
He asks in close conversation
if *you* know whose face at dawn
will lie on the near cushion.

The wife with the new child
wins him because she breeds.
The trees breed long seeds
over the lawn, must or all
is lost, all energy fail,
the daisy, the dog and cat
and brief birds in rain forests.

Here in a corner of the desert
the dark wife bleeds away
his seed into the sand by choice,
washing away with precious water
all change, all chance, all easy access.
His salty sweet taste falls out
of her body—not barren, only empty,
as she wants it to be.

Widow

I have had this lesson,
not to care for the bones.
The cat in my lap dies,
he is replaced, the man who
casts me out is cast out,
the love that leaves returns
as "a wall of water," she kept
saying, as if the words
were the flood and all she could see
she would repeat: "A wall of water."

Wipe me out. I have been replaced,
supplanted, ignored, cast out,
ground down, spat upon, rejected,
refused, neglected, soiled,
reviled, dismembered.
I have lost husband and children,
beasts and possessions, I am ashes,
an orphan; my dearest self took a gun
into himself and died in the fields.

My breasts are empty pockets.
Pain visits my body; tears
my eyes, my mouth is filled
with wind, I speak nonsense
incessantly, silence is fled
from me, wisdom hides her head.
A feverish energy holds, then drops me down.
My children flee from me. A succession
of bruises bloom on the long bones of my body.

Oh God of the waters, God of the fragile body,
imperfect and weak,
watch over me, care for me,
raise me up out of the plumes of the dust,
the rusty canyons.
Rinse and nourish me. In return I have
nothing but my great and perfect
need.

Visitant

You're such an old person
to stand on tiptoe in position
at my window.
But I'm not in my chair. I'm in the country
shearing sheep. A nursery character.

What do you want?
It's *not* lonely here, or in the city.

I've got power? Yes, of a sort,
like my mother's, small feet in their fur boots
high heels (she was short and vain) and tied
with blue ribbons. In snow she walked fast if she could,
her only sport. In summer simmered
on the front porch.
Three times a day she changed stockings,
real power in those days in a city,
pure silk in short supply.
What did she do with money? She hoarded
for her husband who spent it on "business."
What's that, do you suppose? Not sin.
Power? I don't think so.

Sometimes I have trouble swallowing. Don't laugh.
The politics, even that artist I've known twenty years
come round to say he's "fallen from power"
because *his* friend, our senator, decided to retire.
Sometimes it takes away my breath. You smile, yes,
and so do I, running on at the mouth so I can't bend over
this love's broad shaggy back to clip it.
Age is tidy, I've found. My mother's chief worry
was spots on the bosom, that lovely rose silk
with the tie at the throat gone spotted in front
and no help for it, no cleaner to take it out.

Someone will spin this wool into yarn.
She sits in her yard in the shadow of an elm
sipping bark tea when her fingers tire. I help her comb and card
what I bring. Come cold, she'll knit wool thread
into a warm throw I'm about ready to wrap up in,
a bunting to keep away the chill
nights when even the cat won't go out
not to hunt or sniff or call at the window.

I'm through with prowling,
everything gone dry
between my legs but a small burning.
Mother, don't cry.
I don't talk like this much.
Funny, you used to say you felt your mother hovering
ready to advise. Now you call me on your birthday.
Last year you reached your arm out of cloud
to give me a coat. It's over there
in the farmhouse closet, waiting.
Keep yourself warm, you're getting old, you said.

Some Other Women Now

Where did the words go?
Thrown out the window
with grief, that perfume
of rush and obedience;
a collapse with Mother
gone down to the pavement below
and crushed. Blunt trauma.

"Worse," she said, "was the defection
of your father. One Christmas morning
I woke up and he was gone, his mistress,
about whom I knew nothing, installed
in an apartment across town. The tissue
wads still under the tree and you
not born yet, still nudging my rib,
that sore place, with your elbow. Fancy it."

Petticoats, their dark familiar shadows
on the floor after the dance. Rustles
and tangos of taffeta ruffles at the hem.
And crinolines around our shiny knees
over the jellied shine of our ballet slippers,
crimped leather at the toes underneath.
Oh, the dresses: velvet crushed at the armpits,
sleeves for a strapless black bodice
with the creamy brocade. The money they spent
on dancing clothes the year Papa was davening
in the old front bedroom!

Click. A trip to the maternity
ward in deep night. A full moon means nothing only
a son and daughter he claims and won't feed.
Mucus plugs dropped again and again I can't
make sense of all this crippled what for?
The best I can do is continue.

Iced over,
not calling for help (who'd listen), she complained
to the cleaning lady, herself in tears, the keloid scar
at the corner of one eye collapsed on itself. One side
a cheerful disposition, poison the other side, rat trap
to scare away the scurry in the kitchen. Women alone
one after another in wind in streets in air moon fled
moon bottomed bottomed out. Path lost

Poor. Poor kiddos   old crumbs
          on the ground.
The witch watches in her forest, rests a broomstick
          on a turret
cloud. She knows. Her language roils in her throat
          like phlegm
collecting. When she speaks, the syllables spill
like waves on a leap to air. If we're lucky below
          we catch foam.

I Am Sick

"Please." I ask my wife
but she doesn't hear me, I'm lucky.
What I mean is
please make light the window.
Last night
she sewed on my button with wax thread.
"That should hold you," she says,
pulling it through, patting me on the chest
where it leaks and hurts.

In the dark my head feels loose,
emptied, like the coffee thermos
on the sink edge.
I'm all bone. "Not yet," she says
at the curb. Cars, noise, a stink
I don't know. And we cross.

I pick up mail from the box.
I want to. The squares are heavy
from far away, stuck with a taste
on my tongue like paste I try to chew off.
The box is black and flakes
under its sun, a red flag I push up.
"Don't," she says.

"Don't," she says when I hit the dog.
Once it bites me, a ladder of black stitches
on my palm she kisses.
Every day after dinner
behind her back at the sink
a bucket of fire empties.

four

four

Piecing the Universe Together with Dresses

"Do you have many dresses?"
"Yes," I say remembering
the red dress, the green dress,
the marrow-colored jersey tight
across the breast with your names
on the collar. You are coming.

Under flannel my thighs cross.
Under silk my biceps rev up
for moving. If I were smart
I'd begin to sew a shroud,
an oatmeal woolen robe,
a linen wrap for after the bath. Batches of birds
distract me from this.

Somewhere in a square state
workers are starting a building
of rooms with cavernous closets.
Sometime soon, we may go there.
We will undress. We will fill
those closets with dresses.
In the mild air, birds will be singing.
We will bathe in a fountain.
We will lie down together forever
the electric coils of our arms
randomly touching. With the sparks
we will light rooms.

She Speaks

I sit in this summer house
and, Adam, I think of you
and your preposterous naming
and talking, your making the world
new each day—how exhausting—
and the tall banyans you drew up
out of the ground to show me;
each day the tangerine rose-hips,
the azure of an ocean you called
blue, meaning one color, and which
to my eye was *variegated*,
a word you had no use for;
parrots and sparrows you
feathered in one direction
not accounting for the variable
air currents; the rugosa
and its blatant fruit, so
provocative, so showy.

Outside the cottage now
you are no longer here,
a pale basswood flourishes
in all this salty weather
and numerous foliages evolve
nameless in the fresh water
rain. Animals whose plush fur
matts away the damp howl
for attention, beg
to be let into any shelter

but this one, Adam,
a house of women
with no names, only
a companionable silence
that admits no visitors;
only later, perhaps, an orange
presence in a circle of stones,
now like the sun, now the moon,
now flickering, now pausing,
now going soundlessly up.

Detail

with a line adjusted from Ezra Pound

This young woman is hurt
like the rest of us
but for the first time.
She is very thin.
When she is frightened
she goes to the phone book
and opens it at random.
Who do I know whose name
begins here?
She is living at these times
by the principle of the fine
nursery poems that have made her
famous. And she dials, she says,
numbers she hasn't tried in years.
Her voice so calm. She doesn't say
Please help me but says instead
My lover left me. What would you do?
This question they answer in detail, she says,
and detail is what she notices.
It seems to me as we talk
she has grown wise.

When she asks I tell her
the latest painful detail
of my life and she listens:
how the flowers, oh, the colors
of exotics by the ocean
make patterns, colors growing
in layers in circles behind
the wooden houses, and she hears
the names of these wonders

marigold, yarrow, Kansas gayweed,
zinnia, petunia, loosestrife,
wild rose and others,
portulaca and Russian thistle.

Now mind you *I* am not a poet
and not much for detail
except for the catalogue
which more easily represents
a proliferation of confusing detail
in my life: several children
from different fathers, old egg yolk
on dishes, a new person in my office,
the supreme courtroom of our state
whose walls of local wood
say, this is true,
"Eyes and ears are poor witnesses
when the soul is barbarous."
Really it is too much
to expect clarity of detail
when recounting the moment today
when a man stepped
unintentionally I am certain
into my very path
and I, forgetting the many years
of intervening detail,
marriage, assault, divorce,
his lawsuit against me,
patted in passing his belly
with my left hand. This new ring's
gold gathered around it the very light.

I'm certain he noticed.

Oracle

Everything good happens.

Except this: she betrayed me;
Said what I said to a man of iron
powerful enough to ruin me with lightning.
No, not really.
Where I rest in the center, over the earth, is still steady.
I'm paid to twirl in the steam and speak riddles and I do,
often enough to please the togas. They need me.
But to my women I say truth plain, straight
as their hems brushing dust in our courtyard.

I'm given wine every hour and mostly I'm quiet
until the yard fills. That woman served grapes
between chantings when my throat failed and the ache
under my ribs spread. She could tell by my flailing.

She gave what I said away.
My vision melted and ran down her arms
from her mouth, blind colors all salt-scattered,
what fixes my swing over the earth gone suddenly lax.
She sweated for days. They wrapped her in linen towels
but no good. I'd chanted vowels alone, a sullen token
from the InnerGods. They're fallen,

As I am, torso wrenched to one side of my sling.
When I feel better, the hooves gone from my head,
the temple empty and my chin dried off by wind,
I'll come from this cave of hair and my dung
to sing her healthy. She's sick now. No woman of mine
could betray me. And the man? Tomorrow

I'll know. They feed me corn gruel as the steam thickens.
It helps my digestion. The Gods are waiting.

Pregnant Woman

Whose husband is gone, take your daughter by the hand,
lead her to the window where the widow is framed,
raking her leaves. That woman is bowed down by fall.
Say, "We're not as she is, daubing her lips, blowing
out of our noses the dry dust. We have taken control of weather."

Make the sun rise. Raise up wind, mother of changes,
who lives in your mouth. Let the bellows of your lungs rest
on this infant's head, a fulcrum on which to balance the force
of your wind, a colorless rush through your halls
to rinse carpets, raise dust in corners, shatter glass
from the breakfront. Let the corners of furniture splinter.
Take from your armpits electricity of desire,
comb it through your hair and the hair of your daughter.
Sparks from her blonde head ignite your dark one,
the night moves off, see, you are doing it, she is doing it.

Woman of power and movement, woman who knows life
moving in your body, life passing through you like water,
the kitchen faucet you turn on full, washing potatoes,
turning their bottoms up under splashing water,
water the cushion, water the soother, water
the cleanser, you are water
and wine, you are
electricity, the power
you push into the world
when the muscles of your body clench hard
and you pour new life.

Rub your belly with ashes, with pumice,
sweet oils of clove and anise to glisten
on the round of your belly, reflect
sunrise and sunset, keep that fire intact.
You the water and the myrrh, sulfur you are
and strong smelling, strong tasting, elemental preserver,
golden in your powerful spasms and flashings.

Sabbath

Sick with woman's blood and wanting
to mix flour and salt with egg and milk
I make instead this story of Mary,
a pale Jewish girl at the moment
her robe turns raiment. Still and waiting.
I am told by a gentile to envision
that girl myself, newly touched
critic of women's poetry come
to writing in terror on tiptoe.

He says we're all come from bodies
of women, aren't we,
yourself a woman speaking in tongues,
(headachy)
your blurblings very like the cat's?
Your menses, the pauses and circumlocutions
of ordinary speaking, only a way of pushing
some door most of the way shut?

How am I Mary, whose womb shut long ago
against interruption just in time to get
this work done with my mind, slamming
shut her office door?

Day finished, I go to my kitchen for breadmaking
put on the apron of my service, fold the temple
pieces of my eyeglasses closed and hope
facing the frosted window
to hear open into place wings
lifting the golden braids by yeast,
the whisper of unfolding linen,
clipped eyelet edges,
the click of the spice palace opening its pierced sides
silver
odorous
gleaming.

Small Shelter

The needful things have been done:
sugar in the cupboard, honey, sweet
bacon in the smokehouse; buckles
done up, pines felled by lightning
shored against the flood bank.
Nothing to do now but wait.

I got to a tin box, remove
your ring, bed it for some long
season. Oh love, we have risked
our lives for this and still
it is over, long shadows crossing
over us. Fold, hands, be still for the sake of memory,
for our sweet sake who have done
the needful things, who have been true
to our hands, to our hard shoring up.
No floods can take us now.

I braid up my hair, our tent,
that sweet shelter.
Now winter.

Pain

On the windy patio
all the spring of that marriage
we talked.
At dusk, torrential rain
flooded the plains
to hex in summer.
By autumn it was over.

Another summer I wake in the quiet
to pain filling my chest with such a water
as I must drown; wake, pull up
and say its name out loud
into the humid air. Sweat pours
that later I sponge off
in case my emptied body
offend its shroud; I must die for it.
I say your name.
But no, you rise and put your hand,
exactly pain-sized, on the place
and rub it down.
Though what you touch is only skin,
some vessel deep within
lets go, a crack, and drains.
I whisper something,
touching back, and for a while
can breathe, and float, and stroke,
and live.

A Meeting with My Ex-Husband

You are well,
could be said
to be taking it well:
solid scar tissue.
You have lost 24 pounds in 22 days
you say over lunch,
a circle of greens.
You have had some money,
have bought a new bike with the money,
some gold, Cartier watches, two
color TVs, an electronic alarm,
some Gucci things with the money,
a pair of imported somethings.
You are nowhere in trouble, you say,
flipping through
the new albums. You play
me some music about a Halston
dress, about a classy
child, about traveling far.
A pomander on the display
case is left over from Christmas.
All its winking is gone, ribbons,
sweet scents, no proof against
contagion.
        Oh Lord.
I sit and obediently watch
Old Hawk, most radiant of creatures.
What can I, who myself am fallen,
do with such a crashing?

When I can go
I do go out
into the air
and annihilating sun.
It burns and promises
to peel me down
from the quick
to the bone
and I go home.

High Ground

I am on my knees planting my garden.
The tulips are ivory bulbs, safe now
in onionskin as I bury them.

They grow all winter, February, March
snow breaking. I chase away the dogs.

The first one crests
broken but red, so bright
in the sun its bending should be
brief and simple.
I watch it fade through the window.

Stake it,
you advise, stake it
my books say
so I do, string sudden on a wooden paddle.
The veins in the petals threaten to open wide
and spill.

But it stands
and soon I am watching it
shine. Now the second
shows pale below the shoulder
of the first. Bare strong buds
at its stem flare wide at the bottom
where they gather.

My cats are black and tan and lie on the broken earth
sharing sun that warms into summer
the old lilies.

With Stanley Kunitz at the Car Wash

Just as the boy with round pink glasses
takes my money and waves me into line,
a voice on the radio says what sorrow teaches.
I turn up the volume on the car speakers.

As the wide felt streamers jiggle past
the windscreen and over the top,
he talks about dying: like sex,
that informs the work of a boy in his twenties,
death comes into the work of an old poet.

And he *is* old, says the announcer
whose voice rises with the music
between commercials. Jets squirt
soapsuds around the wing vents
I daub up with a damp Turkish towel
someone shoved in the door before.

At talk of his father, a suicide,
something metal grinds at my expensive
aluminum: a flaw in the system
my car passes over, then back onto
the straight and narrow track again,

just as Stanley's voice rises
in joyous affirmation of fig trees
and shoe lifts, and we burst out of the dark
and go dripping but shining
back into the city's traffic.

five

five

Advice

Let's not begin with the body.
Let's put it in a chair, there,
ready to process its clickings
and boomings, dogwood or *My Sin*,
its cheekbones under fingers,
pizza or caviar at all-night places
whose lots are every color marked
in puddles. It will leave us alone.

Let's proceed, instead, through the veil
to a place without color, whose pearly
knots have meaning *sans* referent,
borrowing it only later, and in a way
we don't need to market or do anything
about, without consequence or spinning.

Restraint

Where you have come before me in the field
between the maple windbreak and the sky,
stands straight, now swaying, a pole ridge pine,

its needles stiff with wind-bristle and cardinals
that on the ground tuck into each other's beaks
plump seeds, some evidence of spring and snow-melt;
it meets the horizon at the level where you flex

your beautiful, wide knees to crouch and examine
the minute particulars of stem and needle-leaf.
You, whose voice rouses deeply the wind

to swinging, to fingering lips, cheeks, the curve
of head rounding to its airy palm,
touching and retouching your shining, pale hair,
thick-blowing in sun and moving with wide breath . . .

I take you in,
hold you,
breathe and exhale you.

Journal Entry [The Tropics]

Today was hot.
A morning of packing and cleaning
and sitting on the lanai high over the city.
Papaya for breakfast and Kona coffee.
The Manoa cloud kept close. No rain.

With Caroline I went to the fabulous
snorkeling beach whose creatures are on display
under the surface of the water.
She brought masks.
We climbed the black rocks instead,
thin women in black
swimsuits of the same fabric,
one fair, one so dark
I wear stars in my ears.
We sat by a man-sized oval piercing
in the rocks on either side of a cleft
in the rocks that whirled and filled
and overflowed in our laps
jets of sea water.
Such salt.
"I want to lick the undersides
 of those rocks," she said,
 that beautiful woman,
"close-pored," as the man
 would say at whose side
 I have spent some happy nights, now over.

People took our picture.
Some sand nearby was olive-green,
olivine from the lava. Inside
the cracked, volcanic rock
were light strands called Pele's Hair.
We said we'd meet again.
We touched and parted.

At night after a meal
of raw fish, sashimi, I fly home
to this freezing.

Friend in a Distant City

Touch me.
The flesh is absurd
its veils and encumbrances.
The thin membrane
the cat's eye shelters in
is perfect, while we,
with tears in our eyes from twigs,
want only to be petted,
our eyes closed with kisses
only the soul knows how to give.
They brush from the corners
those tatters of longing
with no color we name
pearly or *blush*.
We are imperfect,
ridiculous.

So on a morning
I woke to light fingering
plush curtains, felt
the floor touch
the warm soles of my left foot
now my right as I pushed
into action under a pale lawn
nightgown. Where you were,
in another city, you got up
naked, the same light streaming
over your dark shoulders, oiling
them into muscles the soul delights
in touching on its daily round
through the body. Oh Soul.
Come forward.

Sex

The white dove in your house perches on my finger
when you touch her breast. The sound she makes!
—now babies nursing, now women coming.

In your garden the floodlight you hold strokes
rows of feathery carrots; dahlias fill up
their cages, tomatoes sprout through upright tubes,
the fluted shoots of your peppers. Corn rows
your son planted poke up soil in a grassy mulch.

The stars are cold and shivery as we touch.
O, put your palm on my shimmering backbone
in its silky trough. It wants you to.

Alone

It is late at night.
I am drinking hot milk.
I dip my fingers in it
          and suck them:
Breasts giving a sweet, thin
          milk to you.

My hand is on you, under your hand.
Your hand is on me, under my hand.
Close, you say
and I hear you.
Close, I answer
and you hear me.
Later where we come together
tips and fills.

How the moon dilates and swells,
          love,
How generously she spills her light
through my window!

On the sill, willow branches
          tap and still, tap

I cup my palm to my face:
You there, with me.

How hungry I am, suddenly
          love,
How quickly I have forgotten
these words.

Look

anywhere. Someone more
beautiful follows with eyes
the color of caramel, the color
of denim, cornflower, topsoil,
overtone of carmine, new leaf,
hair the color of bittersweet,
patent leather. Over your shoulder
should you choose to look
she lolls on the grass
sunning, her tongue on *loose*
her eyes closed, no wrinkles
shouting *age age* at the corners.
Bow to her. Whisper, "nice day"
whisper, "my own brown tree"
say "love me, love me,"
and see how her shoulder dips
to you, all the sudden
hollows filling with silver
wide eye flicking open
then shutting askew
on one color, your color:
a sliver of bone
a sluice of water, running.

Lacunae

Commercial questions we call them, questions
of disease, disuse, questions of nobody's
business. Disgusting. Everyone knows
the fabric they're cut from. Everyone warns us.

Cautious, I set out for the new city.
City of closed gates, she calls it,
Cool city. Wind rises in pines,
in cypress. Rounding the river bend,
the bright road passes the salt flats,
bright mica chips for surface, a sprightly
balance. I am traveling faster. See,
I am going the long distance.

Companion, will you leave me here
having taken me beyond fear, the flat
places, into mountains? We should both
be sorry to lose what we have lost:
night noises, susurrus.

Some doors are curtained. Ascending
the stairs requires bending. You have fallen
flat to greet me. Palm to palm we . . .
I will open. I will

Never forget this place, this price,
this proud house in the clearing. I will never
Yes. It is time to go for food.
See how the light brightens in the windows,
see how the wind rises again, air freshens,
sun, sun come to me here, come here I am

C3

On the human brain: "It didn't really evolve for the purpose
of trying to understand the space time continuum or look
at things in a hundred thousand dimensions. It was there
to keep you out of the rain and help you figure out where
the berries are."
The Mathematician Roger Graham,
quoted in the *New York Times Book Review*

The galaxy discovered
tonight on the news
is a fitting celebration of a promotion
from what I've been doing to what I'm doing.
So this galaxy is touted as new,
a recent birth twelve million years ago.
We buy it.
One galaxy with star cluster to pin on our pocket.

Vanity and personal affection: pin point
clusters to distinguish us from the idiot
girl on the corner, handing over bunches
of paper flowers to the man in charge.
Folks left her there on the curb
holding tight to what seems fashionable now,
blooms on wire stems, slightly drooping
in fresh water fog, hardly snow.
Not pathetic.

Tonight on the telephone you called to check politics.
Cool and polite, you indicated just what you wanted
in code and I, being quick (which justifies my promotion),
picked it up and spoke back. Berries and rain.
Shelter. You heard me, all right.

Tonight I speak as a man who works wood with his hands,
yes, a woodcutter gathering raw materials for fire.
Or a man in the rain with sharp tools,
steel he mounts in a frame of teak.
He planes rough places to straight.
I work with my arms until they ache, my hands hurt,
the spoiled places under my nails blacken with fester,
berries of pus that spurt out the splinters
if I'm patient. I'm patient.

God came to me as a child. I was a child and spread myself
a film of rain to give birth on. Long ago the earth spoke flesh,
I heard, deciphered berries and shelter, and Oh God, I lay back
and then I gave birth.

Dotted Swiss curtains move in sun,
breathe in and out wind I bathe my face in,
bathe my face in a still room, the warm air
unmoving until the furnace coughs on. A sough, a sigh.
Be still. Hear the cicadas begin their wire song,
that heat in the ear. Now see the cicatrix under leaf fall.
Overhead trees whisper their code. If I'm patient I hear
birds moving in code they care nothing about.
Be still. Speak nothing but silence.

Ambition

suits-up in ruffles,
doubles at the waist;
one foot circles behind
in a fluent gesture; dips
the chin down and smiles
at the camera, eyes fringed.

God makes the mails
through which come invitations,
letters of introduction,
peach parchment with messages,
come over, sit right down,
check here, seal up,
send out, pass through
the brass gates to heaven.

Oh how we want to believe
in the power of stars
in deepest night; even seasons
of familiar breezes, flora—
the pesky varieties of insect
in the copper screens of the back porch.

So we remember in print
long afternoons on cretonne chaises,
reading aloud to cousins from one volume
after another familiar adventures: mice
in ceramic suits, darning-flies flickering
in deep recesses of the Chippendale
wardrobe that lets-on alleys, paved
with golden cobblestones that buy . . .

whatever it is ambition wants, that deceiver,
leaking scents at the public occasions
where we star, standing straight
as a parent dictates, looking ahead
into lights, eyes watering for the sake
of all our adventures, all our brain-cells
strutting together, telling old news.

Helios at Bread Loaf, the Album

In these pictures
the sun is so good to our faces
erasing the fissures, easing pressure
on sinuses, unstoppering ears!

In this photo
we gambol like goats in the mountains
and here we are resting on steps
drinking beer.
The sun does it all, fueling us, calling us
out of our casings, unmufflering us.
Our smiles attest to it.
Our legs are bared to it; hair falls
to our shoulders — so much heavy hair,
sun on it, sun priming us,
sun triggering us.

Explosion
behind the forehead unloads
words, works of the arts, parts
of a general legacy. Such
delicacy of feeling, layering
of attitudes, fiery connections
soldered intelligently together.
See how chapters emerge, poems,
tricks respected by critics of stamina.
We all carry papers.

See how we clasp hands
before the bush laden with berries,
three graces heady with wine, groggy,
transported to the dining room.
We smile, heavy-lidded, at the camera,
part of a gathering of images
for the book,
still unwritten.

The Man

I know a man
with a bird in his throat.
Sometimes he opens his mouth
to sing.
It sings.
Sometimes he gags
and I watch.

Why I am interested
who can say,
liking only
the occasional song:
icycles
(as some kid wrote)
or *rope*
made into occasional robes.

When he drips,
an audience in Chicago
watches the puddle
forming at his feet;
he calls it, "The Middle West."
Sometimes the bird
splashes, chirps
Sandhills and *Platte*,
sometimes other names
of far mountains
and the climbers
who bring back
rhododendrons
for the wealthy.

Everything on TV he watches
and the bird
makes it into music.

Some men are born with a big
mouth
and the hinge for opening up wide.
The dentist loves him
and certain young lovers
from among the academic classes.

In the meantime
the sounds from high trees
attract me: some
birds not caught
in a throat. How they sing.

My Dream, Your Dream

In half-light salt
crusted in my eye
corners but I haven't
been weeping, only
traveling in a country
where you come careening
around a corner on your bicycle, wind a wall
you've smashed into,
far side of your face
gone flat on the bone.
I reach to wake you up
to me but you say *no*
and turn into a half-light
of your own, hair a crest
on the pillow and you're
heading into blue rain
rising fast over the windy
crescent of some western hill.

September   [Getting Married Again]

In the night of the long day
On which we have driven five hours
To find your father,
Who has prodded and measured us,
And we, afraid,
Have said *this one* to the gold bar

In miniature, for the rings,
And he has promised to make them;
At midnight, on that night,
Cold and afraid, wakeful,
I come to the kitchen.

In the midst of a welter of china
My children have dirtied in the course
Of their bodies' nurture—
In my absence, yellows and reds
Crusting the sides of dishes—
Is the cardboard box
Your mother has filled
For our pleasure:

A butternut squash in the shape
Of our body; onions
So rich a purple they are royal;
Their papery brothers;
The orbs of fall tomatoes,
Scarlet, rimmed with gold
And capped by a green star;
And dull green apples
Round beyond compass measure,
Pure white at their center,
A perfect fullness of flesh
That taken hold of and opened
Will make our eyes water.

Prospectus

Time to order
the disorder:
task:
an electrifying novel
in which the hero
is seen to have lived
fully clothed in lies,
to have loved
in solitary
and so is penalized.

A non-fiction account
of the trial in which
his old partner
takes to task
his rival for doing
what he did, but slower.

A couple of couples
drink sweet drinks
all summer, growing
thinner and tanned;
the world pivots
on the jut of their hip bones.

Told from the vantage
of the hip bones,
it might catch fire
and generate money.

The cheekbones of the lovers
rub in a most convincing way.
On film, their oiled skin,
the sheen, can stand for another
more explicit encounter.

Or a book of poems
whose sexual and political power
rivets each to the roiling teak deck.

A bestial encounter
in violets
behind the house,
the thread narrative.

The only immutable:
a surgeon's knife
opening swiftly
the chest of a son.
His heart leaps
into focus
at the very moment
the brother's brain
meets the bullet.
Blood in tubes
and basins.

Clear mask
as the small head
rises, falls
back into the hands
of strangers.
The audience is riven.

From terror
comes action.

In the garden
easy flowers,
the marigold and daisy,
flourish in the season
of tomato blight.

What is the reason?
History is a nightmare
from which we can
never awaken. Source:
another better novel.

To kneel and rock
in autumn
on cliffs
over the bay—
the *auteur* wants to be lowered
to the water on ropes,
wants to be learned and just,
unlike the others,

and swims away.

Atonement

Dear God of silence for women,
God, absent from bath and laundry room,
God, whose clotheslines on rainy days
never droop wet linen, look on this flesh,
this heavy head, and take pity
on those of us who neither rejoice
in the burn unit for another day's suffering,
nor insist on our worthiness in the halls
of power. What do we know,
who wrap our wet hair in towel turbans?

Bless a daughter in the distant academy
who stains her tissue samples with Toluidine Blue O,
watching under her microscope the group tissue turn magenta,
and bless the daughters who hunger not
for food, but only to subdue their bodies.
Forgive us the great sins of our fathers, and
of our flesh, and wanting knowledge,
for which we are punished by a ceasing of hunger;
and for the greater sins of the heart
that lead us away from familiar men.
Let us be free of them, except sons
and lovers and those who write well.

God, it's raining tonight on the day of the fast.
The dog next door is groveling in his yard.
Someone I love has a broken heart;
it can't mend, it won't be grafted on.

Those who are dead and melted in the boneyard
and those newly come there, or coming,
who rest on their chrome stretchers in the hall
scarcely breathing, or not at all, who
wait for the scalpel and the blood basin,
let those be filled with silence but for the dripping,
the rustling of wrens hushed in dark.

Let me be worthy of keen hunger,
of ambition, and not afraid past bearing
of all that you offer and take away.
Let my eyes open in the morning
and my body raise me up
to my feet. And let my feet move
in particular service to all who revere you and worship
the world. And then let me leave it.

Bear

The bear inside lies down.
The fire gutters.
Winter comes on
fields deer browse in,
hunters' guns a hollow muffle
we hear from ditches we scour
for grasses, dead husks
without seeds to transport.
Geese overhead, wing tips silver
against blue flats, steel sun
glittering off icy branches, a ricochet
of splitting color lancing lids.
Eye pupils contract, black pinpoints without choice
light will enter, will enter.

Version

Let me be better than
yellow at the window,
wind blowing a hat to the ground,
yellow hat with spent veiling.

Let the birds sing at a distance,
vulgar birds with their holes
and feathers. Let the children
sit on a bench under the espaliered
bushes, their glossy frost shapes
caught between pyracantha thorns.

Where are the parents? Sitting on lawn
covered chaises in their creamy linens,
drinking champagne. It's the right color.
And the sun? Overhead in all seasons.
And the beasts? Frolicking in the grass,
snouts to mole furrows. And the rain?
Seeping into basements where mushrooms
grow in beige cases on the carpet.

Scavenger, get to work. You have strength
and will to do it.

Inside the Geese

an alarm clock is ticking.
I can hear it so I stop my car
by their muddy field.

They are resting, now listening
to the noise my car makes, its engine idling.
They are poised on their mainspring,
wings ready to spin out with tension.
They don't care where I'm going.
But now, the waves they are
begin to rise slowly
line on line rushing to air
moving as if they are air
that cools the ticking metal of my car.
They rise, I press my foot
into the accelerator to drive
down this road to a new school,
watching in my mirror
the geese settle into sky.
My time is up. They take
themselves from the heavy earth
I move across,
heart ticking again and again and again.

Life Outside the Self   [The Uncertainty Principle]

In air, scratched portholes
canted to the stiff balloon sides
on which drops flatten in patterns,
air holding water close in thin film
without color:
only a sort of proof
that the closer you are to data
the less they show anything.

I'm told all this is the consequence
of looking, and the very ground and field
of modern physics, a subject
that used to kill off its practitioners
if they, turned forty, hadn't detached
one brilliant fragment from the whole mosaic.

The Times says, now (a more modern age)
they work in concert, just another team,
each one a plonk in the music of the tin bucket
at a corner of the exploding sunflower field,
slowly filling with soft water as of now
an unspecified composition
without a frame (though closely studied here),
and every kind of color.

Acknowledgments

Acknowledgment is given to the following for the first
publication of some of the poems in this volume: *North
American Review, Denver Quarterly, Poetry Miscellany,
The Pennsylvania Review, Plainsongs, Earth's Daugh-
ters, Whole Notes,* and the anthologies *Alternatives:
An American Poetry Anthology; All My Grandmothers
Could Sing;* and *Forty Nebraska Poets.*